A

Literature Unit

for

Shadow of a Bull

by Maia Wojciechowska

Written by Michael Shepherd

Illustrated by Theresa M. Wright

Teacher Created Materials, Inc.
P.O. Box 1040
Huntington Beach, CA 92647
©1992 Teacher Created Materials, Inc.
Made in U.S.A.

ISBN 1-55734-411-6

Table of Contents

Introduction

A good book can touch our lives like a good friend. Within its pages are words and characters that can inspire us to achieve our highest ideals. We can turn to it for companionship, recreation, comfort, and guidance. It also gives us a cherished story to hold in our hearts forever.

In Literature Units, great care has been taken to select books that are sure to become good friends!

Teachers who use this unit will find the following features to supplement their own valuable ideas.

- Sample Lesson Plans

- Pre-reading Activities

- A Biographical Sketch and Picture of the Author

- A Book Summary

- Vocabulary Lists and Suggested Vocabulary Activities

- Chapters grouped for study, with each section including:
  - *quizzes*
  - *hands-on projects*
  - *cooperative learning activities*
  - *cross-curriculum connections*
  - *extensions into the reader's own life*

- Post-reading Activities

- Book Report Ideas

- Research Ideas

- A Culminating Activity

- Three Different Options for Unit Tests

- Bibliography

- Answer Key

We are confident that this unit will be a valuable addition to your planning, and hope that as you use our ideas, your students will increase the circle of "friends" that they can have in books!

Sample Lesson Plan

Each of the lessons suggested below can take from one to several days to complete.

LESSON 1

- Introduce and complete some of the pre-reading activities on page 5.
- Read "About the Author" with your students. (page 6)
- Introduce the vocabulary list for SECTION 1. (page 8)
- Ask students to find definitions for these words.

LESSON 2

- Read Chapters 1 and 2. As you read, place the vocabulary words in the context of the story and discuss their meanings.
- Choose a vocabulary activity. (page 9)
- Ask students to design a plan for conquering their fears and implement the plan! (page 11)
- Work in groups to dramatize the street scene in Arcangel. A number of variations are possible. (page 12)
- Discuss the book in terms of geography. (page 13)
- Begin "Reading Response Journals." (page 14)
- Administer SECTION 1 quiz. (page 10)
- Introduce the vocabulary list for SECTION 2. (page 8)
- Ask students to find definitions.

LESSON 3

- Read Chapters 3 through 6. Place the vocabulary words in context and discuss their meanings.
- Choose a vocabulary activity. (page 9)
- Make gazpacho. (page 16)
- Research people, places, and customs of Spain. (page 17)
- Discuss Spanish words related to bullfighting. (page 18)
- Discuss a new sport, its rules, and vocabulary. (page 19)
- Administer SECTION 2 quiz. (page 15)
- Introduce the vocabulary list for SECTION 3. (page 8)
- Ask students to find definitions.

LESSON 4

- Read Chapters 7 through 9. Place the vocabulary words in context and discuss their meanings.
- Choose a vocabulary activity. (page 9)
- Make a cape; practice matador's moves. (page 21)

LESSON 4 *(cont.)*

- Calculate the education and cost for several career choices. (page 22)
- Discuss the book in terms of cattle raising. (page 23)
- Discuss "sneaking out" at night. (page 24)
- Administer SECTION 3 quiz. (page 20)
- Introduce vocabulary list for SECTION 4. (page 8)
- Ask students to find definitions for these words.

LESSON 5

- Read Chapters 10 through 12. Place the vocabulary words in context and discuss their meanings.
- Choose a vocabulary activity. (page 9)
- Discuss health and sports risks. (page 26)
- Categorize jobs according to the level of risk. (page 27)
- Draw a bull in a bullring. (page 28)
- Discuss role models students look up to. (page 29)
- Administer SECTION 4 quiz. (page 25)
- Introduce the vocabulary list for SECTION 5. (page 8)
- Ask students to find definitions for these words.

LESSON 6

- Read Chapters 8 through 15. Place the vocabulary words in context and discuss their meanings.
- Choose a vocabulary activity. (page 9)
- Create a vocabulary game. (page 31)
- Act out a favorite scene. (page 32)
- Discuss medical careers. (page 33)
- Discuss the relative importance of life decisions. (page 34)
- Administer SECTION 5 quiz. (page 30)

LESSON 7

- Discuss any questions your students may have about the story. (page 35)
- Assign book report and research projects. (pages 36 and 37)
- Begin work on a culminating activity. (pages 38 through 41)

LESSON 8

- Administer Unit Tests: 1, 2, and/or 3. (pages 42, 43, and 44)
- Discuss the test answers and possibilities.
- Discuss the students' enjoyment of the book.
- Provide a list of related reading for your students. (page 45)

Before the Book

Before you begin reading *Shadow of a Bull* with your students, do some pre-reading activities to stimulate interest and enhance comprehension. Here are some activities that might work well in your class.

1. Predict what the story might be about just by hearing the title.

2. Predict what the story might be about just by looking at the cover illustration.

3. Find out if students have heard of Maia Wojciechowska, and if they know anything about her personal life or her writing.

4. Are you interested in:

    —stories that take place in a foreign country?

    —stories about taking risks?

    —stories about being afraid of something?

    —stories about helping friends?

    Would you ever:

    —sneak into a bull ring at night?

    —consider a dangerous career?

    —attend a bullfight?

    —say "No" to something that many people wanted you to say "Yes" to?

    —help a friend achieve his/her goals?

    Have you ever been unsure of what career you should choose when you grow up? What are some jobs you might really like to do?

5. Work in groups or as a class to create your own book of challenging things to do.

About the Author

Maia Wojciechowska was born in Poland, but when she was still a teenager, she fled with her family to France to escape the Nazis during World War II. She later saw her first bullfight in Spain, while awaiting entry into England.

One afternoon, when this headstrong teenager was told to stay in her room, she slipped away to watch the famous bullfighter, Manolete, display his bravery in the ring. At that moment she became a lifelong aficionado, a real bullfight fan.

Eventually Maia arrived in the United States and attended high school and college. She married and had a daughter, Orianna, but never lost her interest in bullfighting. Once, while traveling in Mexico, she fought a bull herself to the cheers of local residents and was awarded the ears and tail of the bull.

Later, visiting Spain, she met a boy who helped her create the character of Manolo Olivar in *Shadow of a Bull*. As she says:

> *He had a face with a long nose and very sad eyes, and he stood in a bar behind a counter that reached to his mouth. The upper part of his face looked very much like Manolete's when he was that age.*

Wojciechowska became worried that the old men at the bar would pressure the boy into becoming their new bullfighter-hero. Her worries became the beginning of *Shadow of a Bull*.

Maia Wojciechowska's interest has not been simply to publish an interesting story, but to help young people face the problems of growing up and of learning when to remain firm in their own ideas and desires and when to give in. She knows that all young people have choices to make and the price they must pay for any choice they do make.

Under the name Maia Rodman, she has written *Market Day of 'Ti Andre* (1952), another novel for young people and *The Loved Look: International Hair-styling Guide* (1960). Under the name Maia Wojciechowska, she published many other works for young readers. Her *Odyssey of Courage: the Adventure of Alvar Nunez Cabeza de Vaca* (1965), recounts the historical wanderings of a Spanish explorer in Texas, Mexico, and the Caribbean. His adventures with the Indians for seven years can captivate young audiences. Her other writings include *The Life and Death of a Brave Bull* (1972) and an adaptation of *Tuned Out* which became "Stoned: An Anti-Drug Film," (1981) starring Scott Baio.

(Quotations for this biographical sketch taken from "Maia Wojciechowska," p. 3, Atheneum Publishers)

6

Shadow of a Bull

by Maia Wojciechowska
Macmillan, 1964

Available in Canada from Collier Macmillan of Canada

Manolo Olivar, a young boy living in the small town of Arcangel, Spain, has a big problem. Manolo is the son of Spain's most famous bullfighter, Juan Olivar, and everyone in Arcangel expects Manolo to be a brave bullfighter like his father.

But Manolo is not brave. He is a coward. He is afraid to ride a bike, swim, or jump out of a wagon. Too ashamed to tell anyone that he is not a "macho" young man, Manolo lets the six leading men of Arcangel groom him for his first bullfight, an event scheduled to take place even before Manolo becomes twelve years old!

The frightened boy wonders whether he should, in spite of his fears, really become a bullfighter. He is unsure of himself but practices nightly with a muleta—a kind of cape that a matador waves at a bull. He makes friends with an older boy, Juan García, who wants to fight bulls so badly that he sneaks into pastures at night to make passes at them with a cape. Juan and Manolo sneak into the bull ring at night. Later, Manolo sees firsthand what can happen to a bullfighter when he visits "El Magnifico," a young man gored by a bull's horn. Manolo meets a friendly doctor and helps him stitch up El Magnifico's badly torn leg. The son of Juan Olivar, still uncertain about a career in the bull ring everyone else expects him to follow, awaits the fateful tienta, his first bullfight.

On the day of the tienta, Manolo talks to Alfonso Castillo, who, although he wrote books about bullfighting, was too frightened to be a bullfighter himself. Manolo dutifully enters the arena and bravely faces the bull for a few minutes, but then tells all his supporters who are pushing him to be like his father that he does not want to be a matador. Manolo urges his backers to help out by assisting his friend, Juan García, who desperately wants to become a famous torero. Juan then enters the ring and impresses the crowd with many beautiful passes with the cape. Manolo is content to renew his acquaintance with the doctor he met earlier and study medicine.

Vocabulary Lists

On this page are vocabulary lists which correspond to each sectional grouping of chapters. Vocabulary activity ideas can be found on page 9 of this book. Many of the definitions are found in the "Glossary of Bullfighting Terms" at the back of *Shadow of a Bull*.

SECTION 1

Chapters 1-2

coward	matador
resemblance	tienta
torero	prophecy
legend	hero
bullfighter	cathedrals
corrida	biography
summon	gypsy

SECTION 2

Chapters 3-6

fiesta brava	cafe
picador	bull ring
olé	veronica
toro	cape
agility	shrine
disgraced	montera
banderillero	dedication

SECTION 3

Chapters 7-9

fiesta	mass
saeta	ganaderos
toss	jealous
earnestly	aficíon
brave	proximity
horn	epidemic
toril	groves

SECTION 4

Chapters 10-12

gored	honor
penicillin	miserably
fascinated	passes
self-doubts	seriousness
basin	amputation
amonia	endure
museum	incompetent

SECTION 5

Chapters 13-15

disappointed	paralyzed
prayer	decision
pride	portrait
unafraid	caress
amazement	magnificent
nostrils	chicuelinas

8

Vocabulary Activity Ideas

You can help your students learn and retain the vocabulary in *Shadow of a Bull* by providing them with interesting vocabulary activities. Here are a few ideas to try.

- ❑ People of all ages like to make and solve puzzles. Ask your students to make their own **Crossword Puzzles** or **Wordsearch Puzzles** using the vocabulary words from the story.

- ❑ Challenge your students to a **Vocabulary Bee!** This is similar to a spelling bee, but in addition to spelling each word correctly, the game participants must correctly define the words as well.

- ❑ Play **Vocabulary Concentration**. The goal of this game is to match vocabulary words with their definitions. Divide the class into groups of 2-5 students. Have students make two sets of cards the same size and color. On one set have them write the vocabulary words. On the second set have them write the definitions. All cards are mixed together and placed face down on a table. A player picks two cards. If the pair matches the word with its definition, the player keeps the cards and takes another turn. If the cards don't match, they are returned to their places face down on the table, and another player takes a turn. Player must concentrate to remember the locations of words and their definitions. The game continues until all matches have been made.

- ❑ Have your students practice their writing skills by creating sentences and paragraphs in which multiple vocabulary words are used correctly. Ask them to share their **Power Vocabulary** sentences and paragraphs with the class.

- ❑ Ask your students to create paragraphs which use the vocabulary words to present a **History of Bullfighting** that relates to the events mentioned in the story.

- ❑ Challenge your students to use a specific vocabulary word from the story at least **10 Times In One Day.** They must keep a record of when, how, and why the word was used!

- ❑ As a group activity, have students work together to create an **Illustrated Dictionary** of the vocabulary words.

- ❑ Play **20 Questions** with the entire class. In this game, one student selects a vocabulary word and gives clues about this word, one by one, until someone in the class can guess the word.

- ❑ Play **Vocabulary Charades**. In this game, vocabulary words are acted out!

You probably have many more ideas to add to this list. Try them. See if experiencing vocabulary on a personal level increases your students' vocabulary interest and retention!

Quiz Time

1. On the back of this paper, write a one paragraph summary of the major events in chapters one and two. Then complete the rest of the questions on this page.

2. What is Manolo's problem? _____

   _____

   _____

3. In what ways does Manolo look like his father? _____

   _____

   _____

4. How did Juan Olivar die? _____

   _____

5. What was the gypsy fortuneteller's prophecy about Juan Olivar? Did it come true? _____

   _____

   _____

6. List three things about Manolo that showed he was too fearful to be a bullfighter.

   _____

   _____

   _____

7. Describe the six men of Arcangel in one well-written sentence. _____

   _____

8. On the back of this paper, tell one thing you were afraid of and why you are not afraid of it anymore.

What Are You Afraid Of?

Manolo was afraid of bullfighting. He was afraid of other things, too. He did not like swimming, biking, or jumping from high places. He did not want to get hurt.

Do you think you could learn to be brave in a difficult situation? Overcoming fear and learning to face up to difficult situations is part of life. Here are some ideas to help you get started.

What is something you are afraid of but would like to face up to?

_____

_____

Why is it important for you to overcome your fear of this?

_____

_____

Who would help you conquer your fear? Would you have to do it all by yourself?

_____

_____

What is the first thing you need to do to master this fear?

_____

_____

How long will it take before you are not afraid anymore?

_____

_____

Would it have been better for Manolo to just avoid swimming, bicycling, jumping, and bullfighting? Why?

_____

_____

Would it be better for you to simply avoid the thing you fear? Why?

_____

_____

Act It Out

Manolo Olivar was not a "macho" young man. Not only was he afraid of facing a bull in the ring, he didn't do things that other boys did when they were playing—swimming and bicycling.

When he was nine years old, he was walking home from school when two things happened on the same day to show him that he was not brave. When the other boys of Arcangel saw a broken hay wagon, they immediately took turns jumping off the pile of hay and onto the grass. Manolo couldn't jump off the tall stack of hay. He was afraid.

The same day, Manolo was crossing the central plaza of Arcangel when he was embarrassed a second time. He jumped back from a passing car and fell backward into the gutter.

> *"It was four in the afternoon in the plaza with his father's statue at its center. The men who were always sitting at the tables of the cafe were all there as usual. As he fell, he heard them laugh."*

The men tell him never to jump back, to be like his father. When Manolo got up, he wanted to run away and hide, but the men made him sit with them and talk about bullfighting. Here the six men begin training him to be a bullfighter.

Groups of students can act out this scene. Each group may do it a bit differently. You may change the outcome if you wish.

Possibilities include:

- Manolo can talk out loud about his feelings. (For example: *"That haystack is pretty tall. I think it's too tall to jump from."*)

- Kids and other bystanders can tease him about being afraid.

- One of the six men could argue with the others about whether Manolo should really try to learn bullfighting.

- Manolo could jump off the hay wagon and hurt himself.

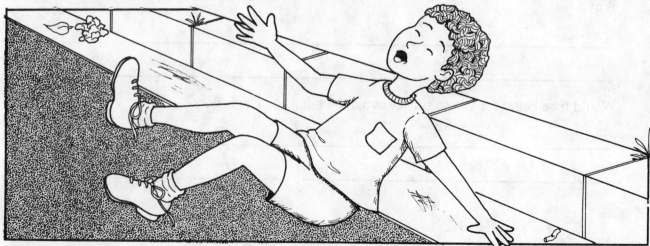

Geography

Manolo Olivar lives in Archangel, a fictional town in Spain. Spain is a real country and the Guadalquivir River is a real river in the southern part of the country. Seville is a large town on the Guadalquivir, and to the northeast of Seville, also on the river, is the town of Cordoba.

Use a wall map, a map from the encyclopedia, a social studies text, or an atlas to find the places on the map below. Label them.

Madrid	**Guadalquivir**	**Bay of Biscay**
Cordoba	**Portugal**	**France**
Seville	**Pyrenees Mountains**	**Barcelona**
Mediterranean Sea	**Andalusia (region)**	**Valencia**
Atlantic Ocean		

Reading Response Journals

One great way to insure that the reading of *Shadow of a Bull* touches each student in a personal way is to include the use of Reading Response Journals in your plans. In these journals, students can be encouraged to respond to the story in a number of ways. Here are a few ideas.

- Ask students to create a journal for *Shadow of a Bull*. Initially, just have them assemble lined and unlined three-holed paper in a brad-fastened report cover, with the blank page for the journal's cover. As they read the story, they may draw a design on the cover that helps tell the story for them.

- Tell them the purpose of the journal is to record their thoughts, ideas, observations, and questions as they read *Shadow of a Bull*.

- Provide students with, or ask them to suggest, topics from the story that would stimulate writing. Here are a few examples from the chapters in SECTION 1.
  — Manolo looks like his father; everyone says so. Describe how you look like someone else or at least how people say you look like someone else.
  — Manolo was afraid of bikes, swimming, and high places. Tell about some of the things you are afraid of.
  — People expect Manolo to be like his father. Do people expect you to be like your father or mother? In what ways?

- After the reading of each chapter, students can write one or more new things they learned in the chapter.

- Ask students to draw their responses to certain events or characters in the story, using the blank pages in their journals.

- Tell students that they may use their journals to record "diary-type" responses that they may want to enter.

- Encourage students to bring their journal ideas to life! Ideas generated from their journal writing can be used to create plays, debates, stories, songs, and art display.

Allow students time to write in their journals daily. To evaluate the journals, you may wish to use the following guidelines.

- Personal reflections will be read by the teacher, but no corrections or letter grades will be assigned. Credit is given for effort, and all students who sincerely try will be awarded credit. If a grade is desired for this type of entry, grade according to the number of journal entries completed. For example, if five journal assignments were made and student conscientiously completes all five, then he or she should receive an "A."

- Non-judgmental teacher responses should be made as you read the journals to let the students know that you are reading and enjoying their journals. Here are some types of responses that will please your journal writers and encourage them to write more.

  "You have really found what's important in the story!"
  "You've made me feel as if I'm there."
  "If you feel comfortable, I'd like for you to share this with the class. I think they'll enjoy it as much as I have."

Quiz Time

1. On the back of this paper, write a one paragraph summary of the major events in each chapter of this section. Then complete the rest of the questions on this page.

2. Manolo watches his first bullfight and receives a gift from the matador. What is it?

    _____

3. What is an aficionado?

    _____

4. Name three kinds of bullfight fans and explain each.

    _____

    _____

    _____

5. The six men are trying to teach Manolo all they know. Is he learning? Why or why not?

    _____

    _____

6. What is Manolo doing at night that he is not supposed to do? Why?

    _____

    _____

7. Count de la Casa talks to Manolo. What does the Count tell him? How does Manolo feel after that?

    _____

    _____

    _____

8. Manolo is learning how to be a bullfighter, but is not sure he wants to be one. Have you ever had someone try to teach you something you were not sure you wanted to learn? Explain on the back of this sheet.

9. Some people do not think bullfighting is a good sport because of the suffering of the animals. What do you think of the sport?

    _____

    _____

    _____

Gazpacho

Andalusia, the region of Spain in which *Shadow of a Bull* takes place, is known for its foods, especially fried fish, Jabugo ham, and wines such as amontillado, which has a hazel nut flavor, and moscatel, which is a sweet raisin wine.

A typical food is *el gazpacho*, which is a popular summer dish. Gazpacho is a cold vegetable soup. It is prepared in several different ways and usually consists of bread, oil, garlic, water, and tomato. Other ingredients such as cucumber and fresh pepper are often added to it.

As a class project try preparing some gazpacho. Follow the recipe below dividing up the ingredients and any necessary equipment for preparation. Fresh ingredients work best, but canned may be used. Serve croutons along with the soup.

Gazpacho
(Cold Vegetable Soup)

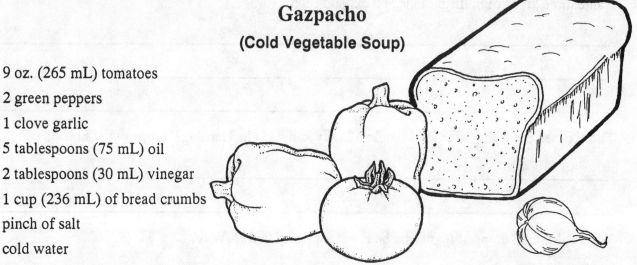

9 oz. (265 mL) tomatoes

2 green peppers

1 clove garlic

5 tablespoons (75 mL) oil

2 tablespoons (30 mL) vinegar

1 cup (236 mL) of bread crumbs

pinch of salt

cold water

Peel and crush the garlic. Take the seeds out of the peppers and chop. Cut tomatoes into small pieces and add bread crumbs. Mix everything together and add olive oil a little at a time, stirring continuously. When the oil is absorbed, add cold water and then strain it off. Add vinegar and a pinch of salt. Serve cold.

More About Spain

Spain is a very different country from the U.S.A. A small town in Spain, like the town of Arcangel described in the novel, may be very different from a big city. Spain also has different customs and places to visit.

Work in groups of two or three. Discuss the list below and decide which ones to research. Use encyclopedias, reference books, atlases, and other research materials. Share your findings with the class.

CITIES

- Seville
- Madrid
- Cordoba
- Bilbao
- Zaragoza
- Cadiz
- Barcelona
- Castille
- Valencia

CUSTOMS

- pesetas
- saeta
- pundonor
- Gabriel
- Catholic
- fiestas
- St. Veronica
- harvest
- gypsies
- La Macarena

PLACES

- Andalusia
- Granada
- Pyrenees
- Crete
- Morocco
- Guadalquivir
- Gibraltar
- Portugal
- New Spain

BULLFIGHTERS

- Belmonte
- Manolete
- Gaona
- Lalanda
- Chicuelo

Spanish Words

Shadow of a Bull contains many Spanish words that are used to describe a bullfight. Write the letter of the phrase in the in the right hand column next to the word in the left hand column that is describes.

1. _____ *fiesta brava*   A. pass with a cape

2. _____ *veronica*   B. carry sticks to hook the bull

3. _____ *aficíon*   C. gate where bull enters

4. _____ *matador*   D. bullfighter

5. _____ *muleta*   E. small cape waved at the bull

6. _____ *olé*   F. carry spears

7. _____ *faena*   G. bull

8. _____ *montera*   H. love of bullfighting

9. _____ *toro*   I. shouted at bullfight

10. _____ *banderilleros*   J. bullfight

11. _____ *toril*   K. bullfighter's hat

12. _____ *picadors*   L. right before the kill

Play Ball!

The six men took Manolo to see his first bullfight and explained everything to him, from the first procession of men and horses into the ring, to the actions of the bull, to the picadors, and the banderilleros and the matador. Manolo learns the important parts of the fiesta brava.

Suppose you were taking a friend to a football game for the first time. Could you explain each step of the action? Here are some parts of the sport to include in your explanation:

national anthem	first down
coin toss	touchdown
kick-off	field goal
first quarter	extra point
half time	2 minute warning
penalty	yard lines
pass	run
block	tackle
quarterback	offense
defense	cheer

Here are some other choices. Describe every aspect of the sport from start to finish. Pretend that your audience knows nothing about the sport. Pick a sport that you know.

baseball	soccer
basketball	volleyball
hockey	rodeo
horse racing	car racing
polo	skiing

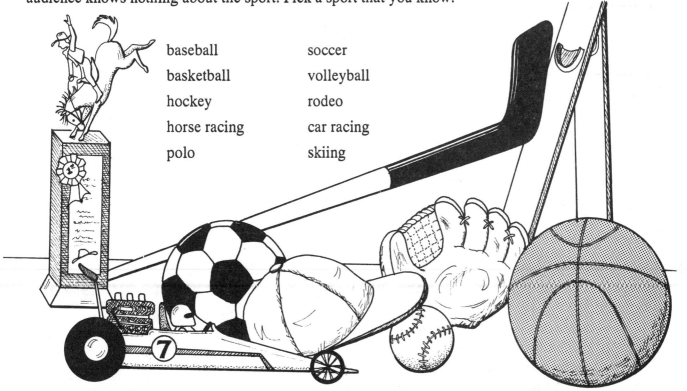

Quiz Time

1. On the back of this paper, write a one paragraph summary of the major events in each chapter of this section. Then complete the rest of the questions on this page.

2. What grows on the land around Arcangel? What animals are raised?

_____

3. What does Manolo try to forget during the fiesta? What do he and Jaime do together?

_____

_____

4. Why does Manolo decide to go to Jaime's house?

_____

_____

5. Who does Manolo talk to when he first arrives at the García home? What does Manolo learn about the family?

_____

_____

6. What does Manolo decide to do to help Juan García?

_____

_____

7. When and where do Juan and Manolo go to practice bullfighting? Was it right or wrong to do what they did? Support your answer.

_____

_____

8. Describe Juan García. Include his age, skills, and attitude toward bullfighting. How is he different from Manolo?

_____

_____

9. How does Manolo save Juan's life? What does Manolo do afterwards that he is ashamed of?

_____

_____

10. On the back of this paper answer these questions and give your reasons. If you were Manolo, would you have:
     a. snuck into a bull ring at night?
     b. invited Juan to the tienta?
     c. avoided bullfighting altogether?
     d. found a less risky way to spend time?

Be a Bullfighter!

Juan García wanted to be a bullfighter more than anything else in the world. You can act like a bullfighter by making a cape out of a piece of heavy cloth, perfectly round with a six-foot diameter. Cut a slit to the middle of the cape.

Practice making passes with your cape:

Chicuelina: the bull passes by the man's side and not in front of him. The man offers the cape to the bull, and as the bull charges, the man makes a pirouette in which the cape wraps itself around his body.

Gaonera: holding the cape behind the man's body and luring the bull past the man's chest.

Veronica: holding the cape in both hands and moving it smoothly in front of the bull and alongside the man's body.

Media veronica: half-veronica. After a series of veronicas the man gathers the cape to one side of his body and the bull makes a very sharp turn following the cape and has to pause.

What Do You Want To Be?

Juan García wants to be matador, just as his father did, but neither one has the money necessary to get started as a bullfighter. Bulls are expensive and training takes time. The six men and Count de la Casa provide all the money needed for Manolo's father and Manolo to become toreros.

What do you want to be? Will you need money to get started? Use books from your school library, pamphlets from your state employment commission, or encyclopedias to find out how much money or education your idea of a future job would require. Work in group of four students. Fill out a chart for each one in your group showing the money, education, and number of years of training required for your job.

Job	Cost for Training	Type of School	Number of Years

You may also be able to get information from your teacher or your school counselor. Someone you know who does the type of job you are interested in might help.

Cattle Around the World

Count de la Casa raised cattle in Spain. His ranch, near the Guadalquivir River in southern Spain, specialized in raising bulls for the popular bullfights, but most cattle production in the world is for meat and dairy products that people use for food.

Below are some statistics that show the number of beef and dairy cattle raised in the ten leading cattle countries of the world. Use these figures to fill in the bar graph on this page. Working in 25 millions, round these figures and then fill in the bar graph.

Country	Number of Beef and Dairy Cattle
India	182,000,000
Soviet Union	117,186,000
United States	115,199,000
Brazil	93,000,000
China	57,450,000
Argentina	53,670,000
Bangaladesh	36,000,000
Mexico	33,873,000
Ethiopa	26,300,000
Columbia	24,275,000

Number of Beef and Dairy Cattle *(in millions)*

200
175
150
125
100
75
50
25
0

Country

Something You Did One Night

In Chapter 9, Manolo Olivar and Juan García sneak into the bull ring in Arcangel so they can practice their bullfighting skills. They climb a fence and make a few passes with the bull. Juan has a close call when the bull tosses him up in the air, but Manolo helps lure the bull away from his fallen friend.

Answer these questions, sharing the answers with teachers or classmates only if you feel comfortable doing so.

1. If you were Manolo, would you have gone illegally into a bull ring? Why or why not?

   _____

   _____

2. Have you ever been asked to sneak out at night with someone? What did you say?

   _____

   _____

3. If someone asked you to sneak out tonight and do something without your parent's knowledge, what would you do? Why?

   _____

   _____

4. Have you ever done something brave to help someone else? Were you surprised that you could do it?

   _____

   _____

5. What could have happened to Manolo and Juan when they broke into the ring?

   _____

   _____

6. What could happen to you and a friend if you went out by yourselves without telling anyone?

   _____

   _____

7. What are some things you can do at night with a friend that your parents would approve?

   _____

   _____

24

Quiz Time

1. On the back of this paper, write a one paragraph summary of the major events in each chapter of this section. Then complete the rest of the questions on this page.

2. Two days after Juan and Manolo secretly went to the bull ring, Manolo goes to see the six men. Why?

   _____

   _____

3. Where do the six men take Manolo? Why?

   _____

   _____

4. Who does Manolo meet for the first time? What does he ask Manolo to do?

   _____

   _____

5. The doctor tells Manolo that "The world is a big place." What does he mean by that?

   _____

   _____

6. Manolo is afraid of getting gored at the tienta. What two things does he plan to do to avoid injury?

   _____

   _____

7. Why does one of his plans fail?

   _____

   _____

8. Manolo thinks that his father might have been afraid. Where does he go for information? What does he find out?

   _____

   _____

9. What offer does Manolo make to Juan? Does he accept? Why or why not?

   _____

   _____

10. If you were Juan García, would you have accepted Manolo's offer? Explain your answer on the back of this paper.

Hazardous to Your Health

Manolo did not find a warning label on the bull ring that said: "Danger: Bullfighting can kill you! Bulls have sharp horns that can be deadly!" Manolo knew all too well that a bull killed his father. He saw what a bull's horn can do when he visited the young circus bullfighter, "El Magnifico," and watched the doctor sew up the long gore wound in the boy's leg.

Many physical problems can be avoided if people will pay attention to warnings. For example, fewer people would run the risk of death from heart disease or lung cancer if they would simply heed the warning labels on cigarette packages.

Look through some magazines. Find several different cigarette ads. Look at the Surgeon General's warnings. Are they the same in all the ads you found? Write them down.

_____

_____

_____

What does the Surgeon General's warning mean? Write it down here.

_____

_____

_____

In the space below, create your own new warning label for a cigarette ad. Remember it must be short and direct. Check an encyclopedia or other reference book to make sure your warning is accurate.

Job Choices

Manolo Olivar is under a lot of pressure to choose the dangerous profession of bullfighting because his father had been a famous bullfighter. Manolo isn't quite sure, at age eleven, what he really wants to be.

What kind of profession would you choose? Here is a list of jobs. In groups of three or four, decide which jobs are the most dangerous, somewhat dangerous, and not very dangerous at all. Then, individually, decide which ones you would consider as realistic possibilities for yourself.

Job	Most Dangerous	Somewhat Dangerous	Not Very Dangerous
doctor			
lawyer			
preacher			
soldier			
test pilot			
accountant			
nurse			
lion tamer			
salesperson			
politician			
artist			
dentist			
actor			
clerk			
professor			
scientist			
boxer			
magician			
sailor			
homemaker			
auto assembler			
chef			
writer			
football player			
firefighter			
computer programmer			
singer/musician			
teacher			
business manager			
police officer			

Art

Manolo is afraid of bulls, especially the horns that can gore deeply into a man or boy and kill, as a bull had killed his father. In an encyclopedia, find out how big fighting bulls grow to be and draw a picture of one.

Make sure to include the horns, nostrils, hooves, withers, tail, and eyes.

For a humorous look at bullfighting, get a copy of *The Story of Ferdinand* by Munro Leaf (Viking, 1936). Use the funny portraits of the bull, the picadors, the matador, and the crowd to make your own illustrations.

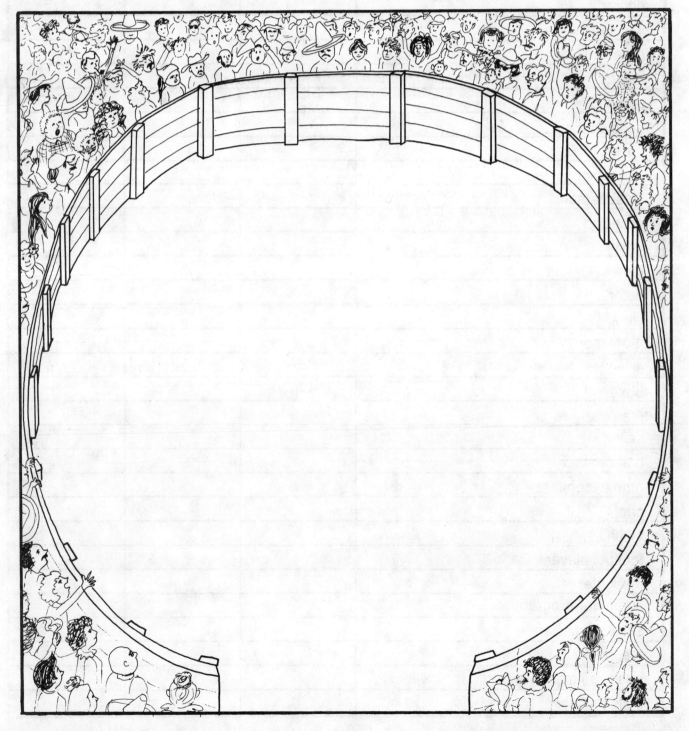

Someone To Look Up To

Manolo admires the doctor: "As he watched the magic way the man's hands brought torn flesh together, he thought that what the doctor was doing and had done was the most noble thing a man could do." Manolo, eleven years old, looks up to the older man. The boy uncertain about his future, wishes he could be like the old doctor: confident, self-assured, helping others.

1. Who do you look up to? Why would you like to be like that person?

   _____

   _____

   _____

2. Sometimes an older person can offer advice. The doctor gently urges Manolo not to throw his life away on bullfighting. Is there an older person you can go to for advice? Who?

   _____

   _____

3. Manolo also looks up to Juan García as a kind of "big brother" who can help him out. Juan is fourteen, brave, and confident. Do you have an older brother or sister or older friend that you look up to? Why?

   _____

   _____

   _____

4. Manolo offers to let Juan take Manolo's place at the tienta, but Juan refuses. Have you ever offered something special to a friend who refused? What was the offer?

   _____

   _____

   _____

5. Manolo looks up to the doctor and to Juan García. Which person has a greater influence on him? Are you influenced more by kids a few years older than you are, or by an adult that you look up to? Why?

   _____

   _____

   _____

Quiz Time

1. On the back of this paper write a one paragraph summary of the major events in each chapter of this section. Then complete the rest of the questions on this page.

2. What does Manolo's mother finally tell him about his father?

_____

_____

3. What does Manolo say in his prayer to La Macarena the night before the tienta?

_____

_____

4. Manolo, Juan, and the six men joke about fear on the way to the tienta. Is Juan afraid?

_____

_____

5. Who is Alfonso Castillo? What does he say to Manolo?

_____

_____

6. How well does Manolo do in the ring with the bull? What mistake does he make?

_____

_____

7. After losing his muleta, what does Manolo say?

_____

_____

8. What happens to Juan?

_____

_____

9. At the end of the book, who does Manolo talk to? What does he say?

_____

_____

10. Does Manolo envy Juan's success? Why or why not?

_____

Come to the Bullfight!

At the end of the novel, Juan García has every prospect of becoming a great bullfighter. In the space below, design a poster for one of his upcoming fights in Seville. Include his age, home town, and skill.

Special Scenes

Some of the scenes in *Shadow of a Bull* are dramatic and memorable. Can you visualize Juan and Manolo sneaking into the ring at night? Can you see the tension in the conversation between Manolo and Mr. García, or Manolo and Count de la Casa? Can you feel the fear Manolo felt? Perhaps you feel his frustration at being trapped in the image of his father.

There is warm friendship in the talks between Manolo and Juan as well as in the brief words between Manolo and the old doctor. In this activity, work in groups of two to four to select scenes that best represent the group's opinions as you read the questions below. Then choose one scene to act out for the class. Before you act it out, write a paragraph summarizing the scene and why you remember it. Practice acting out with the group. Include a reading of your summary and the reasons for the scene's importance in your group's presentation.

Which of the scenes in the story:

- made you laugh?

- made you sad?

- caused you to think about something you had never thought about before?

- made you angry?

- frightened you?

- upset you?

- made you wonder?

- triggered a memory of your own?

- made you happy?

- could you visualize easily?

- did you reread?

- did you want to share with someone else?

Practicing Medicine

Manolo makes the big decision not to be a bullfighter and talks to the older doctor about studying medicine. Does he make the right choice? Answer on the back of this paper in one good paragraph.

Being a doctor requires many years of study. Use an encyclopedia or a book about doctors to answer these questions:

- What courses should you take in high school to help prepare for a medical career?

  _____

- What classes are you taking now that might help you if you wish to become a doctor?

  _____

  _____

- After a bachelor's degree from college, you will need to attend a medical school. How many years of medical school are required?

  _____

  _____

- What are some other medical careers you could pursue?

  _____

  _____

List the advantages and disadvantages of being a doctor.

Advantages	Disadvantages

Imagine Manolo as a doctor and Juan García as a famous bullfighter. They meet again after 20 years have passed. There has been an accident in the bull ring . . . Write a dialogue between the two characters.

Decisions

Everyone has to make decisions in life. Below is a list of decisions that most of us make. Place a "1" by the decision that you think is most important, "2" by the second most important, and so on, until you finish the list.

_____ what to wear to a special party

_____ to marry or to stay single

_____ what car to buy

_____ who to vote for (president, congress)

_____ what career to pursue

_____ where to live

_____ whether to go to college

_____ which hobby to pursue

_____ who to have as a close friend

_____ which hair length/style to wear

How important is Manolo's choice not to become a bullfighter? Why?

_____

_____

How do you know when you have made the right decisions for yourself on these questions? Which issues may not have only one right choice?

_____

_____

Manolo makes several choices in the book, in addition to his career choice. Name some. Are they important?

_____

_____

Shadow of a Bull is basically about a career choice. Look at the list of choices above. Would you like to read a book in which the main character has to make a different kind of choice that changes his or her whole life? Why or why not?

Any Questions?

When you finished reading *Shadow of a Bull*, did you have some questions that were left unanswered? Write some of your questions here.

_____

_____

_____

Work in groups or by yourself to prepare possible answers for some or all of the questions you have asked above and those written below. When you have finished your predictions, share your ideas with the class.

- How do Manolo's mother and grandmother feel about his decision not to become a bullfighter?

- If Manolo had not been the son of Juan Olivar, would he ever have been pressured to become a matador?

- Will Juan García's father change his attitude about the Olivar family?

- If Manolo had never met the old doctor or never talked to Alfonso Castillo, would he have gone ahead and tried to be a bullfighter?

- Would Juan García make a good doctor?

- What would have happened if Manolo's father were a doctor?

- Will Manolo attend any more bullfights?

- Will Manolo get any financial support from the six men to go to medical school?

- Will the country of Spain ever outlaw bullfighting as a cruel, bloody sport?

- Will doctors, teachers, and scientists ever be as popular as sports stars?

- What would have happened if Juan García had died in the ring when they snuck in at 2:00 a.m.?

- Why does Manolo finally decide against bullfighting?

- Can Manolo be happy as a doctor?

- What will happen if Manolo, as a doctor, has to treat a patient infected with a deadly disease?

- How would the story change if Manolo's father had never died in the ring?

Book Report Ideas

There are numerous ways to report on a book once you have read it. After you have finished reading *Shadow of a Bull*, choose one method of reporting on the book that interests you. It may be a way that your teacher suggests, an idea of your own, or one of the ways below.

- **See What I Read?**

This report is a visual one. A model of a scene from the story can be created, or a likeness of one or more of the characters from the story can be drawn or sculpted.

- **Time Capsule**

This report provides people living at a "future" time with the reasons why *Shadow of a Bull* is such an outstanding book, and give these "future" people reasons why it should be read. Make a time-capsule type of design, and neatly print or write your reasons inside the capsule. You may wish to hide your capsule after you have shared it with your classmates. Perhaps one day someone will find it and read *Shadow of a Bull* because of what you wrote!

- **Come To Life!**

This report is one that lends itself to a group project. A size-appropriate group prepares a scene from the story for dramatization, acts it out, and relates the significance of the scene to the entire book. Costumes and props will add to the dramatization!

- **Into the Future**

This report predicts what might happen if *Shadow of a Bull* were to continue. It may take the form of the story in narrative or dramatic form, or a visual display.

- **A Letter to the Author**

In this report, send a letter to Maia Wojciechowska in care of the publisher of the novel *Shadow of a Bull*. Tell the author what you liked about *Shadow of a Bull*, and ask her any questions you may have about the writing of the book. You might want to give her some suggestions for a sequel! Be sure that your teacher has read it, and that you have made your writing the best it can be.

- **Guess Who or What!**

This report takes the form of several games of "20 Questions." The reporter gives a series of clues about a character from the story in a vague to precise, general to specific order. After all clues have been given, the identity of the mystery character must be deduced. After the character has been guessed, the same reporter presents another "20 Questions" about an event in the story.

- **A Character Comes To Life!**

Suppose one of the characters in *Shadow of a Bull* came to life and walked into your home or classroom. This report gives a view of what this character sees, hears, and feels as he or she experiences the world in which you live.

- **Sales Talk**

This report serves as an advertisement to "sell" *Shadow of a Bull* to one or more specific groups. You decide on the group to target and the sales pitch you will use. Include some kind of graphics in your presentation.

- **Coming Attraction!**

Shadow of a Bull is about to be made into a movie and you have been chosen to design the promotional poster. Include the title and author of the book, a listing of the main characters and the contemporary actors who will play them, a drawing of a scene from the book, and a paragraph synopsis of the story.

- **Literary Interview**

This report is done in pairs. One student will pretend to be a character in the story, steeped completely in the persona of his or her character. The other student will play the role of a television or radio interviewer, trying to provide the audience with insights into the character's personality and life. It is the responsibility of the partners to create meaningful questions and appropriate responses.

Find Out More!

Describe three things you read in *Shadow of a Bull* that you would like to learn more about.

1. _____

2. _____

3. _____

As you are reading *Shadow of a Bull*, you will encounter geographical locations, historical events, diverse people, ways of life that are different from your own, and a variety of animals. To increase your understanding of the characters and events in the story, and to more fully recognize Maia Wojciechowska's craft as a writer, research to find out more about these people, places, habits, and things.

Work in groups to research one or more of the areas you named above, or the areas that are mentioned below. Share your findings with the rest of the class in any appropriate form of oral presentation.

(Check the cities, customs, places, and bullfighters listed on page 17. Include them in your research.)

- Spanish language
- government in Spain
- cattle raising
- cowboys
- fortune tellers
- Columbus
- Plaza de Toros
- Cervantes
- Spain
- opposition
- Portugal
- circus fights
- banderilleros
- faena
- cape

- doctors and medicine
- history of Spain
- bullfighting
- Spain, tourism
- Spain, cathedrals
- vegetarianism
- El Cid
- humor (*The Story of Ferdinand*)
- U.S.A.
- tradition
- Mexico
- picadors
- matadors
- veronica

A Look into the Future

In the next four pages, you will be looking into the future life of Manolo Olivar. Using what you know about the places and character in *A Shadow of a Bull*, project what might have happened to Manolo as he studied to become a doctor. Share these ideas with your class.

Travel with Manolo back to his hometown, Arcangel, fifty years after his tienta. Complete the activity on page 40 and share Manolo's thoughts after 50 years.

Display the completed projects from the culminating activities on a bulletin board. Add other information to the display about Spain by writing or calling the Tourist Office of Spain.

Tourist Office of Spain
1221 Brickell Ave., Suite 1850
Miami, FL 33131
Phone (305) 353-1992

Tourist Office of Spain
8383 Wilshire Blvd., Suite 960
Beverly Hills, CA 90210
Phone (213) 658-7188

The Medical Student: Manolo Olivar

At the end of *Shadow of a Bull*, Manolo talks with the doctor about helping out at his clinic after school. If Maia Wojciechowska had written about this time of Manolo's life, how do you think she might have answered the following questions?

- Do the six men continue to support Manolo's mother?

- What is the hardest thing for Manolo to learn at the clinic?

- How do the other townspeople react to Manolo's new friendship with the doctor?

- What do Manolo and Juan García talk about?

- Does Manolo keep going to bullfights?

- What do Manolo's mother and grandmother say when he starts helping the old doctor?

- What books does Manolo read?

- How does the doctor try to prepare Manolo to become a doctor?

- List the things the doctor lets Manolo do and the things he won't let him do.

- Will Manolo ever see Juan injured in the ring?

- Does Manolo ever wish he had become a bullfighter?

Discuss your ideas for all of these questions. Then, working in size-appropriate groups, choose one question and dramatize it for the class

A Look into the Future *(cont.)*

When Manolo decides to become a doctor, he is sure to notice differences between the lives of a bullfighter in training and a medical student. If you were in his place, how would you compare and contrast them?

Use what you know about Arcangel, the people there, bullfighting, and being a doctor to complete the comparison chart below. Add your own insights as well!

Manolo's Two Worlds		
	Doctor	Bullfighter
Risks		
Educational Advantages/ Disadvantages		
Ability to Make Friends		
Level of Contentment		
Criteria by Which Others Judge You		
People You Make Happy by Your Career Choice		

In which career would you be happier? Why?

_____

_____

_____

A Look into the Future *(cont.)*

"But there was no jealousy because he was sure what it was he wanted to do with his life. And his father's life, bullfighting, would stay a part of him, as it always had been, but in a different way than anyone had planned."

This is how Maia Wojciechowska describes Manolo Olivar's attitude at the end of *Shadow of a Bull*. He is sure that he wants to be a doctor, not a bullfighter. But he is also sure that his father's fame as a bullfighter will always be a part of him.

Imagine Manolo has become a doctor in a big city like Seville and is now visiting his childhood home in Arcangel. What does he experience with his five senses? In the space below, describe a few of the sensory experiences he has as he stands surrounded by his hometown (which was practically a museum to the memory of his father). On a separate piece of paper, draw what Manolo sees in the town square. Add your pictures to the class bulletin board display.

What he sees:

_____

_____

_____

What he hears:

_____

_____

_____

What he smells:

_____

_____

_____

What he tastes:

_____

_____

_____

What he touches:

_____

_____

_____

A Look into the Future *(cont.)*

Manolo Olivar revisits the plaza in his hometown of Arcangel, Spain. There he sees the statue of his father, but beside it there is another statue of Juan García, who has also become a famous bullfighter. Manolo is thinking to himself as he looks at the statue. What is he thinking? Fill in the thought bubble in the picture below. After you have written in Manolo's thoughts, cut out the picture and add it to the culminating activity bulletin board.

Unit Test

Matching: Match these quotes with the characters who said them.

       Manolo   six men   Juan García   Alfonso Castillo   the doctor

1. _____ "I do not think you want to be a bullfighter. I do not think you are like your father."

2. _____ "For now, you'll just listen to us. Listen and learn."

3. _____ "Hand me those gloves...Let's see how good a nurse you'd make."

4. _____ "I am not like my father. I do not want to become a bullfighter."

5. _____ "You will be my very best friend, for life. Because you offered to do something that only a very best friend could offer."

True or False: Write true or false next to each statement below.

1. _____ Juan and Manolo sneak into the bull ring at two in the afternoon.

2. _____ Juan Olivar, a famous bullfighter, was honored in Arcangel.

3. _____ Manolo asks the six men to teach him because he wants to begin his bullfighting career as soon as possible.

4. _____ The doctor and Alfonso Castillo both urge Manolo to make up his own mind about bullfighting.

5. _____ Manolo prays that La Macarena will make him brave.

Short Answer: Provide a short answer for each of these questions.

1. _____ How old is Manolo at the beginning of the novel?

2. _____ How does Manolo's father die, and at what age?

3. _____ Who owns the ranch where the bulls are raised near Arcangel?

4. _____ How does Manolo show his bravery when he sneaks into the ring with Juan?

5. _____ How does Manolo meet the doctor?

Essay: Answer these questions on the back of this paper.

1. Is Manolo a coward or is he brave? Justify your answer with examples from the story.

2. Manolo has difficulty making a decision about his career. Do you think he makes the right decision? Why?

Response

Explain the meaning of each of these quotations from *Shadow of a Bull*.

Chapter 1:   "Now the town of Arcangel was waiting, for that hero had left them a son who was growing up to once again take arms against death. They were waiting for the son to be like his father."

Chapter 2:   " 'Count de la Casa was the first to believe the old gypsy. He took Juan to bullfights with him all the time.' "

Chapter 3:   " 'Don't expect it to be an even contest. The bull must die. Only sometimes, very rarely, does the bull not die.' "

Chapter 5:   "Manolo practiced at night, after his mother had fallen asleep and could not hear him. He had to open the windows wide to clear the room of the smell of mothballs. And he did not dare even light a candle, but would swing the cape, much to heavy for his hands, in the light of the moon."

Chapter 6:   "It was no use, no use to please the Count, no use to ignore the fact that they had all decided, without his knowledge, to cheat him of one year of his life."

Chapter 8:   " 'Well, well, well,' he sang out in a mocking voice. 'The great son of a great father! And to what do we owe the honor of this visit?' "

Chapter 8:   " 'You don't even have *afición*, that Spanish poison which seeps into one's blood and makes an invalid out of the strongest of men? You don't even know anything about that afición that makes one wake up in the morning with one thought: to fight a bull...' "

Chapter 10:   " 'I've grown old looking at wasted lives.' He walked over to Manolo and patted his head. 'The world is a big place,' he said gently."

Chapter 13:   " '... your father was a noble man. A man of honor. A man of pride. He would never do anything he did not really want to do.' "

Chapter 15:   "The animal seemed to shoot out of the darkness, its black skin shining in the sun, its hoofs thundering louder by far than the beating of Manolo's heart."

Teacher Note: Choose an appropriate number of quotes for your students.

Conversations

Work in size-appropriate groups to write and perform the conversations that might have occured in each of the following situations.

- Manolo and Juan decide to sneak away to Seville to watch a famous matador. *(2 people)*

- Sr. García hears about Manolo offering his son Juan a chance to prove himself at the tienta. He visits Manolo to thank him. *(2 people)*

- Manolo overhears his mother and grandmother talking about how fearful they are for Manolo's tienta. He joins the conversation. *(3 people)*

- Manolo is working at the doctor's clinic and forgets to clean one of the instruments. The doctor finds out and confronts Manolo. *(2 people)*

- Manolo looks at the statue of his father late one night in the plaza. He hears his father's voice. *(2 people)*

- The doctor visits the six men to talk about Manolo's future. *(7 or more people)*

- The Count, the six men, and Manolo discuss the tienta after it is over. *(8 or more people)*

- Schoolmates in Arcangel try to get Manolo (age 9) to go swimming, ride bikes, or jump off a haystack. *(3 people)*

- Juan has been gored. Manolo, now a doctor, tends to his friend's wound. *(2 people)*

- A policeman catches Juan and Manolo trying to sneak into the bull ring. *(3 people)*

- A gypsy fortune-teller shows up at Manolo's tienta and tells everyone before the event that Manolo will be a famous doctor. *(2 or more people)*

- Juan Olivar and the bull, Patatero, who killed him, have a conversation about how they died and about Manolo. *(2 people)*

- Two townspeople of Archangel discuss the new statue of Juan García being placed in the plaza. *(2 people)*

- The six men show Sr. García and Juan the new house they have bought for the family. *(8 or more people)*

- Manolo, the doctor, and Sr. García all go to watch Juan at a bullfight. *(3 people)*

- The doctor tries to talk to "El Magnifico" about quitting bullfighting for a safer job. *(2 people)*

- At the tienta, the bull tosses Manolo and Juan rushes out to save Manolo's life by distracting the bull. They talk afterward. *(2 people)*

- Alfonso Castillo is interviewing Manolo for a biography of Juan García that Castillo is writing. *(2 people)*

- A panel composed of a famous bullfighter, an anti-bullfight activist, and a moderator discuss the sport. *(3 people)*

- Write and perform one of your own conversation ideas for the characters from *Shadow of a Bull.*

Bibliography

Bullfighting

Aquaroni, Jose. *Bulls and Bullfighting.* (Editorial Naguer, 1957)

Arruza, Carlos. *My Life as a Matador.* (Houghton, 1956)

Belmonte, Juan. *Juan Belmonte: Killer of Bulls.* (Doubleday, 1937)

Buckley, Peter. *Bullfight.* (Simon and Schuster, 1958)

Cintron, Conchita. *Memoirs of a Bullfighter.* (Holt, 1968)

Conrad, Barnaby. *Fiesta Brava.* (Houghton, 1953)

Conrad, Barnaby. *How to Fight a Bull.* (Doubleday, 1968)

FitzBarnard, Lawrence. *Fighting Sports.* (Saiga, 1983)

Fulton, John. *Bullfighting.* (Dial Press, 1971)

Greenfield, Arthur. *Anatomy of a Bullfight.* (McKay, 1961)

Hemingway, Ernest. *Death in the Afternoon.* (Scribner, 1932)

Jones, Larry. *Tijuana Bullfights.* (Toros Grap, 1969)

Leaf, Munro. *The Story of Ferdinand.* (Viking, 1936)

Marvin, Gary. *Bullfight.* (Blackwell, 1988)

Smith, Rex. *Biography of the Bulls.* (Reinhart, 1957)

Tynan, Kenneth. *Bull Fever.* (Harper, 1955)

Varra, Robert. *Felipe the Bullfighter.* (Harcourt, 1968)

Wojciechowska, Maia. *Shadow of a Bull.* (Miller Brady, 1978)—Filmstrip

Spain and Portugal

Cross, Wilbur. *Spain.* (Children's Press, 1985)

Gibbon, David. *Spain: A Picture Book.* (Crescent, 1986)

Lrizarry, Carmen. *Spain.* (Silver Burdett, 1974)

Lye, Keith. *Spain.* (Watts, 1987)

Martin, Rupert. *Looking at Spain.* (Lippencott, 1969)

Rutland, Johnathan. *Spain.* (Watts, 1980)

Seth, Ronald. *Let's Visit Portugal.* (Burke, 1984)

Seth, Ronald. *Let's Visit Spain.* (Burke, 1984)

Rodeos

Fain, James. *Rodeos.* (Children's Press, 1983)

Harvey, Lynn. *Ride'em Cowgirl.* (Putnam, 1975)

Radlauer, Ed. *Rodeo School.* (Watts, 1976)

Tinkerman, Murray. *Rodeo.* (Greenwillow, 1982)

Answer Key

Page 10

1. Accept appropriate summaries.
2. Manolo sees himself as a coward because everyone wants him to be a bullfighter like his dad, but he is afraid.
3. Tall, thin, with sad eyes and a long, thin nose, he resembles his father.
4. Juan Olivar died in the bull ring as he killed Patatero, a bull.
5. The gypsy said Juan Olivar would fight and kill his first bull at age twelve and fight bulls the rest of his life.
6. Manolo did not like to ride bikes, swim, or jump from high places.
7. Accept appropriate descriptions: bullfight fans, afficionados, backers of Juan Olivar.
8. Accept appropriate responses.

Page 13

Page 15

1. Accept all appropriate responses.
2. The bull is dedicated to Manolo; the oldest bullfighter gave him his dress cape.
3. An aficionado loves bullfights.
4. Tourists, who know nothing about bullfights; *toreristas*, who care only about bullfighters; and *toristas*, bull fans.
5. Accept reasonable answers.
6. Manolo is practicing passes with a cape because he is afraid he can't do them well.
7. The six men want him to begin bullfighting at age 11. Manolo is so angry he wishes he had not been born.
8. Accept reasonable answers.
9. Accept reasonable answers.

46

Answer Key *(cont.)*

Page 18

1. j	7. l
2. a	8. k
3. h	9. g
4. d	10. b
5. e	11. c
6. i	12. f

Page 20

1. Accept appropriate responses.
2. Olives grow near Arcangel; cattle are raised.
3. Manolo tries to forget all about bullfighting. He and Jaime enjoy the carnival games, sing, dance, eat ice cream and cotton candy, find a hide-out, steal apples, go fishing, and talk.
4. Manolo wants Jaime's older brother, Juan, to take him along when he sneaks out to pastures to cape bulls.
5. Manolo talks with Sr. García and finds out that he once worked for Manolo's father but was fired. Sr. García is bitter because he is poor and cannot afford to sponsor his son as a bullfighter.
6. Manolo decides to invite Juan to the tienta, Manolo's first bullfight.
7. The boys sneak into Arcangel's bullring at 2:00 a.m. Legally, and regarding a lack of parental permission, this was wrong.
8. Juan is older than Manolo, very confident of himself, and a natural bullfighter. He has afición—a strong desire to be a matador. Manolo has little of this skill, confidence, and desire.
9. Manolo lures the bull away from a fallen Juan. Later, Manolo secretly vomits from his fear.
10. Accept reasonable answers.

Page 25

1. Accept appropriate responses.
2. He wants to get an invitation for Juan García to the tienta.
3. They took him to "El Magnifico," the comic bullfighter's house to see a goring, a wound from a bull's horn.
4. Manolo meets the old doctor for the first time. He asks Manolo to help him sew up the wound.
5. There are many career possibilities for Manolo other than bullfighting.
6. Manolo plans to pray in Seville at the shrine of La Macarena and to keep his back to the crowd at the tienta so they won't see how far away he is from the horns.
7. The six men do not take him to Seville.
8. Manolo goes to the museum library to read more about his father. He also asks his grandmother. Neither source gives any information about his father being afraid.
9. Manolo offers Juan a chance to fight the bull in Manolo's place at the tienta. Juan refuses because everyone expects Manolo to do it and it is Manolo's opportunity.
10. Accept any reasonable answer.

Page 23

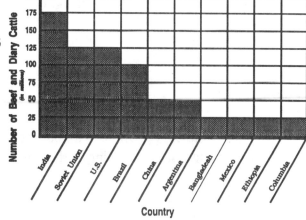

Answer Key *(cont.)*

Page 30

1. Accept appropriate responses.
2. Manolo's father was tired and often wanted to quit being a matador.
3. Manolo prays for courage and safety.
4. Yes.
5. Castillo is a bullfight critic and biographer of Manolo's father. He tells Manolo that he, Castillo, has never fought a bull, and that Manolo should make up his own mind.
6. Manolo does well with the cape but gets the muleta caught on the bull's horn.
7. Manolo says he does not want to be a bullfighter and that Juan García should be given a chance to prove himself.
8. Juan impresses everyone by his performance with the bull.
9. Manolo talks to the doctor and tells him he would like to work with him.
10. No, Manolo is sure he wants to be a doctor, not a matador.

Page 34

You may want to develop a class profile, giving all the *1's* for a particular decision a value of 10, all the *2's* a value of 9, etc., until you can tally up which decisions the majority of the class consider most important.

Page 40 and 41

Create a bulletin board display of these culminating activities.

The board background can be bullfight posters and other materials from Spain's tourist bureau.

Page 42

Matching: 1) Alfonso Castillo 2) six men 3) the doctor 4) Manolo 5) Juan García

True or False

1. False. It was two in the morning.
2. True
3. False. Manolo did not ask. He was fearful.
4. True
5. True

Short Answer

1. Nine years old.
2. His father died at the age of 22 in the bull ring.
3. Count de la Casa
4. He saves Juan's life by luring the bull away from his friend who has been tossed into the air and is lying on the ground.
5. Manolo meets the doctor at "El Magnifico's" house after that bullfighter has been gored.

Essay

1. Accept appropriate responses that use examples from the novel.
2. Accept reasonable responses.

Page 43

Accept all reasonable and well-supported answers.

Page 44

Perform the conversations in class. Ask students to respond to the conversations with questions such as "Are the conversations realistic?" or, "Are the words the characters say in keeping with their personalities?"